discovermore
Exploring Life Science

Life Cycles

Ernest Brazzos

Britannica
Educational Publishing
IN ASSOCIATION WITH
THE ROSEN PUBLISHING GROUP

Published in 2025 by The Rosen Publishing Group, Inc.
2544 Clinton Street, Buffalo, NY 14224

Editor: Brianna Propis
Book Design: Michael Flynn

Photo Credits: Cover Leena Robinson/Shutterstock.com; (series background) Dai Yim/Shutterstock.com; p. 4 Kurit afshen/Shutterstock.com; p. 5 fizkes/Shutterstock.com; p. 6 Daniel Prudek/Shutterstock.com; p. 7 Nikola Bilic/Shutterstock.com; p. 8 Brian A Jackson/Shutterstock.com; p. 9 lovelyday12/Shutterstock.com; p. 10 BlueRingMedia/Shutterstock.com; p. 11 MiguelMartinsDesign/Shutterstock.com; p. 12 Dualororua/Shutterstock.com; p. 13 Matteo photos/Shutterstock.com; p. 15 (top) timsimages.uk/Shutterstock.com; p. 15 (bottom) Luke-diver/Shutterstock.com; p. 16 seasoning_17/Shutterstock.com; p. 17 Catchlight Lens/Shutterstock.com; p. 19 (top) rafaelnpb/Shutterstock.com; p. 19 (bottom) Bachkova Natalia/Shutterstock.com; p. 20 OlgaBartashevich/Shutterstock.com; p. 21 Esmay van Strien/Shutterstock.com; p. 22 K.A.Willis/Shutterstock.com; p. 23 Martin Pelanek/Shutterstock.com; p. 24 Randy Bjorklund/Shutterstock.com; p. 25 Enessa Varnaeva/Shutterstock.com; p. 26 Dragana Gordic/Shutterstock.com; p. 27 terekhov igor/Shutterstock.com; p. 29 (top) Chendongshan/Shutterstock.com; p. 29 (bottom) Colin Seddon/Shutterstock.com.

Library of Congress Cataloging-in-Publication Data

Names: Brazzos, Ernest, author.
Title: Life cycles / Ernest Brazzos.
Description: New York, NY : Britannica Educational Publishing, [2025] | Series: Discover more! Exploring life science | Includes bibliographical references and index.
Identifiers: LCCN 2023051657 (print) | LCCN 2023051658 (ebook) | ISBN 9781641901659 (library binding) | ISBN 9781641901642 (paperback) | ISBN 9781641901666 (ebook)
Subjects: LCSH: Life cycles (Biology)--Juvenile literature.
Classification: LCC QH501 .B76 2025 (print) | LCC QH501 (ebook) | DDC 571.8--dc23/eng/20231222
LC record available at https://lccn.loc.gov/2023051657
LC ebook record available at https://lccn.loc.gov/2023051658

Manufactured in the United States of America

CPSIA Compliance Information: Batch #CSBRIT25. For further information contact Rosen Publishing at 1-800-237-9932.

Contents

Circle of Life 4
Pollination.......... 6
Seeds.......... 8
Bugging Out 10
From Water to Land.......... 12
Underwater Life 14
Hatched.......... 16
Nesting.......... 18
Live Births 20
Unique Mammals.......... 22
Traveling Life 24
Final Stage 26
Unexpected Occurrences.......... 28
Glossary 30
For More Information.......... 31
Index 32

Circle of Life

The circle of life concerns the cycle of birth and death of every living thing. Animals are born, grow into adults that can have their own babies, and later die. The babies grow into adults and have their own young, and so the cycle continues. Plants follow the same cycle, although they reproduce differently than animals.

All clownfish are born male. Only some can change to female for mating purposes.

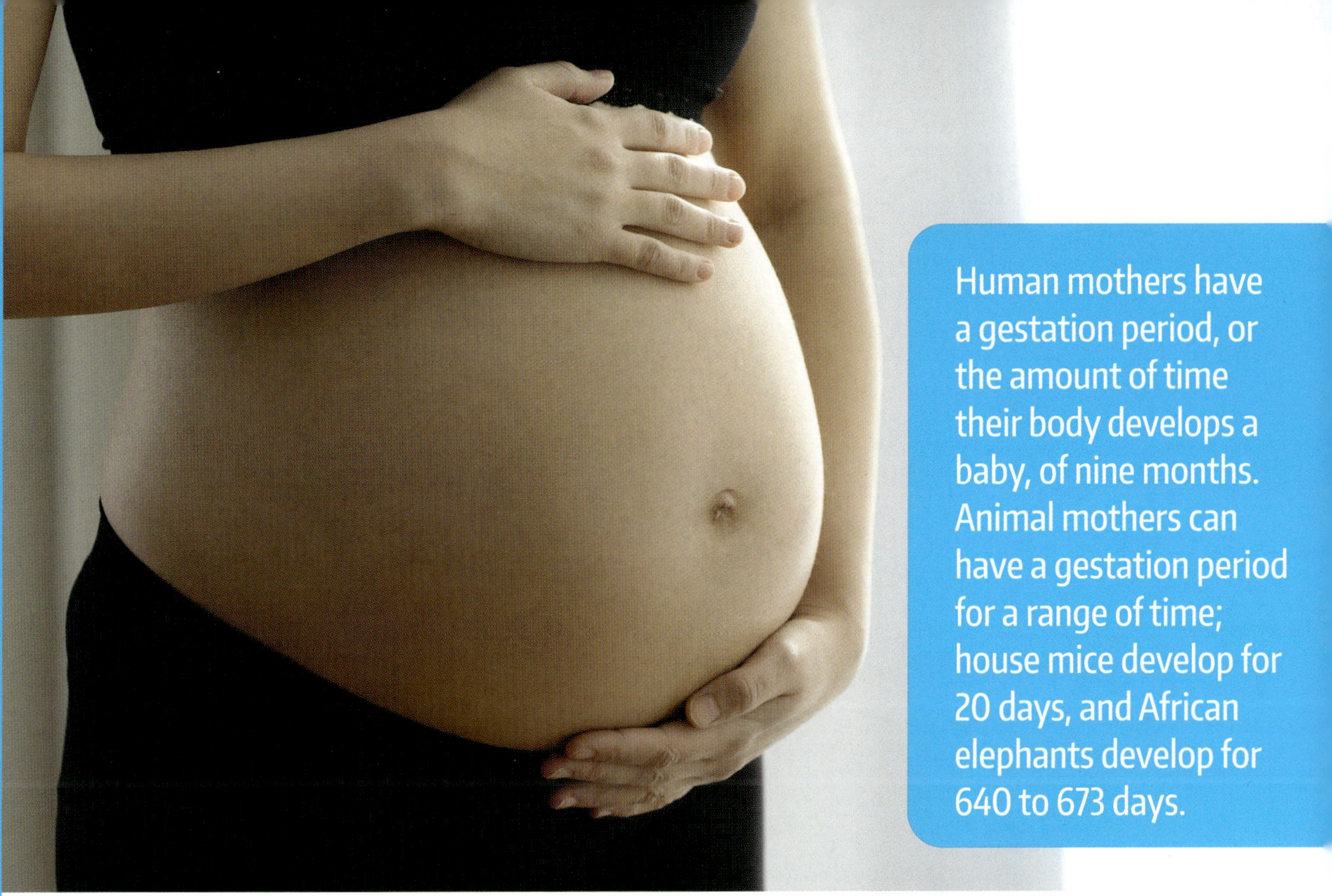

Human mothers have a gestation period, or the amount of time their body develops a baby, of nine months. Animal mothers can have a gestation period for a range of time; house mice develop for 20 days, and African elephants develop for 640 to 673 days.

It's common for baby animals to be small and weak after they're born. They face dangers, such as other animals that want to eat them. As animals grow into adults, they become bigger and stronger. Eventually they have their own babies and can provide for them.

Consider This

When an animal reproduces, they have babies that grow into adults. What would happen if living things were suddenly unable to reproduce?

Pollination

Growing flowers is an important part of some plants' life cycles. Inside a flower there are male and female parts. The male parts make a powder called pollen. When pollen from a flower moves to the female part of a flower, a seed starts to grow in the flower. Seeds can grow into new plants.

Bees play an important role in **pollination**.

When a butterfly feeds on nectar, it helps to move the flower's pollen from one plant to another after it sticks to its body.

Animals can move pollen for plants. Flowers contain a sugary juice called nectar. When birds and bees feed on the nectar, pollen sticks to the animals. The pollen rubs off when the animals visit another flower. The wind can also move pollen from one flower to another.

WORD WISE

POLLINATION IS THE PROCESS OF MOVING POLLEN FROM THE MALE PARTS OF A FLOWER TO THE FEMALE PARTS.

Seeds

Flowers die after seeds start to develop in a plant. Fruits grow around the seeds in some plants. Fruits protect the seeds and help them to spread. Animals eat soft fruits such as berries. The seeds come out in the animals' droppings.

Some seeds, such as burdock, can cling to an animal's fur, which helps to carry the seeds away. They have hooks and spines that stick to the fur.

When a dandelion seed takes flight, its fluff works like a tiny parachute to carry it on the wind.

A new plant sprouts from a seed.

After a seed lands on the ground, it will begin to grow only when the conditions are right. When it's warm and wet, the seed splits open, and the plant starts to spring up. It develops leaves and gets bigger. The plant grows flowers and makes its own seeds once it's fully grown.

Consider This

How do animals and plants work together to produce new plants?

Bugging Out

Many insects hatch from eggs when they're born, but they look different from their parents until they reach the adult stage of life. Beetles, bees, ants, moths, and butterflies go through four life stages: egg, larva, pupa, and adult. This is called **metamorphosis**. They look different in each stage.

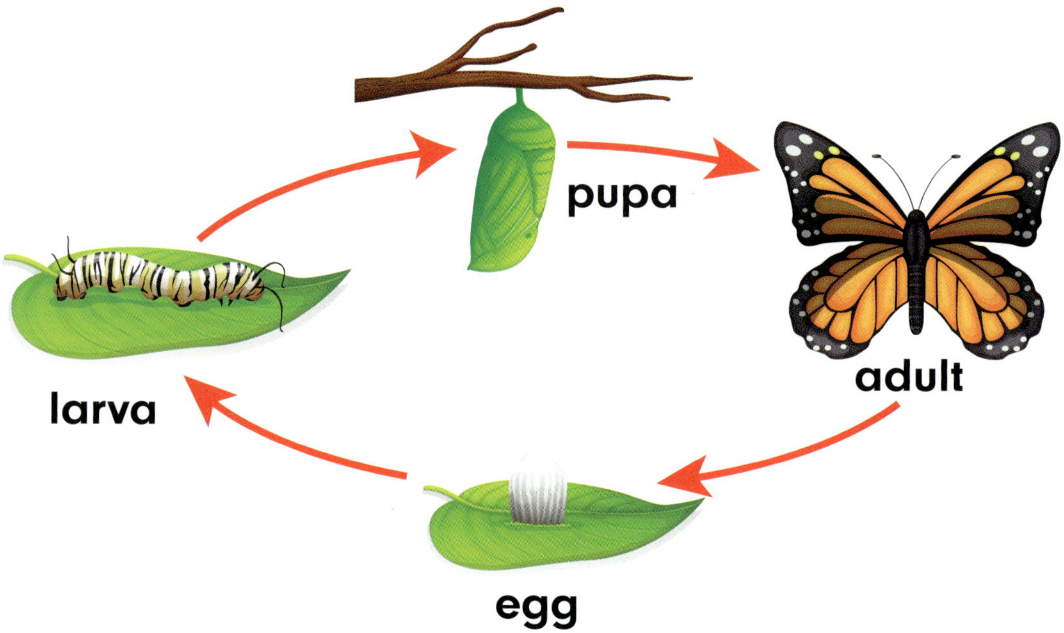

This diagram shows the life cycle of a monarch butterfly.

Baby insects are called nymphs.

Some insects, such as grasshoppers and cockroaches, go through only three life stages. They begin life as eggs. Then they hatch from the eggs, usually as smaller copies of the adults. The insects then grow into adults.

Some insects, such as bees and moths, change by growing wings. Like many insects, bees and moths have four wings. Others, such as flies, have two wings.

WORD WISE

METAMORPHOSIS IS THE PROCESS OF CHANGE AN ANIMAL UNDERGOES TO CHANGE INTO AN ADULT.

From Water to Land

Amphibians, such as frogs and toads, begin their life cycles fully in water. When they are adults, some move onto land though most stay in water. Because amphibians live in water and on land, their natural environments are shores, ponds, swamps, and low-lying meadows.

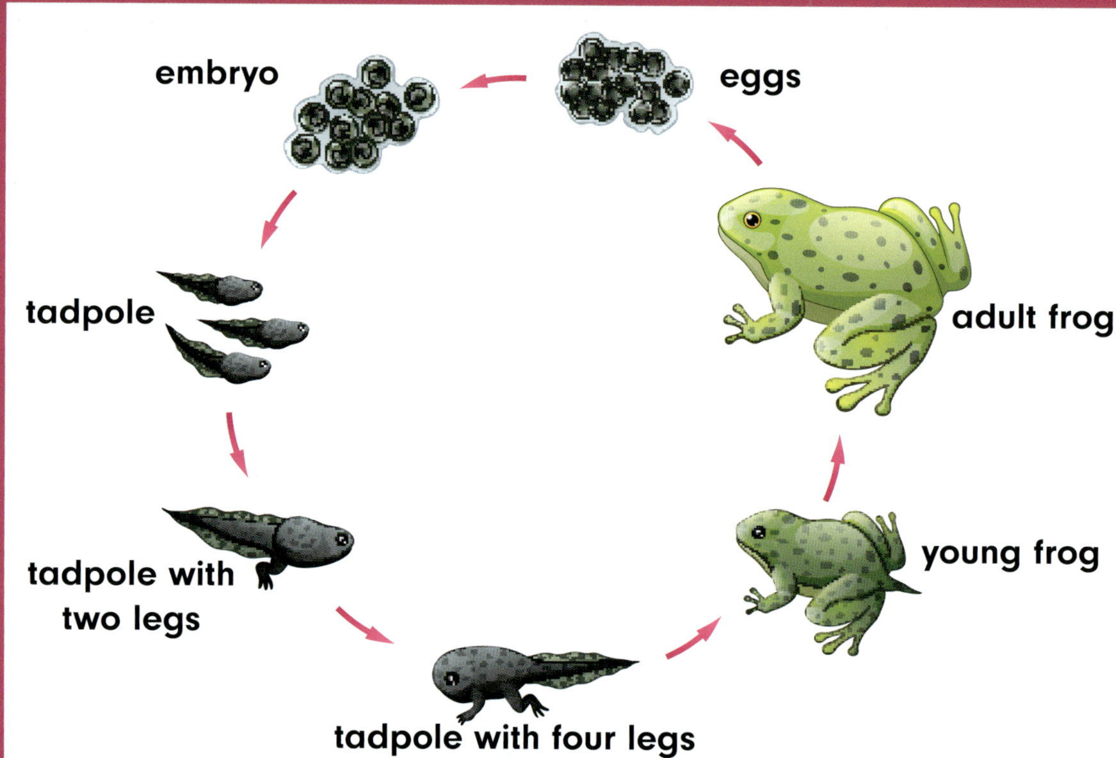

This diagram shows the life cycle of a frog.

Adult frogs live on land and in water. When it's mating season, they move to ponds and wetlands to lay their eggs.

Frogs lay thousands of eggs, usually in the water. After a few weeks, tadpoles hatch out of the eggs. The tadpoles have no legs, and they have a tail. They eat algae, underwater plants, and sometimes other tadpoles.

A tadpole's body changes a lot from the time they're born. First, they grow back legs and lungs and come to the water's surface to breathe air. Then, they grow front legs and lose their tail, becoming frogs. The cycle begins again when the adult frogs lay eggs of their own.

Consider This

If a tadpole lives in water, why do you think it begins to grow legs?

Underwater Life

Fish live their entire life cycles underwater. They begin life as eggs that hatch underwater. Some fish lay as many as a million small, soft eggs. Some fish lay eggs that float on the water's surface or stick to a riverbed. To protect their eggs, fish lay them among plants or rocks to keep them out of sight from hungry animals.

Not all fish guard their eggs—some swim away immediately after laying them. The young fish that hatch out of the eggs grow up alone. At first, they are very small and can't swim fast, so many are eaten by other animals. They are less likely to be eaten when they are older and stronger.

A male jawfish keeps eggs inside its mouth until they hatch.

compare and contrast

How might a fish egg's survival rate differ based on whether they're guarded by parents?

Although male fish will guard their eggs, it doesn't stop them from occasionally eating some!

Hatched

Reptiles, such as crocodiles, turtles, and snakes, reproduce by laying eggs. The eggs contain a yolk for food, but **embryos** also need to be kept warm and safe. Sea turtles crawl onto beaches and bury their eggs under sand. Alligators lay their eggs under a pile of plants. As the plants rot, they create heat for the eggs.

Turtles lay their eggs in the sand to keep them warm. The baby turtles make their way to the sea after hatching.

Mother crocodiles carry their babies in their mouth. They can carry as many as 15 babies at once!

After hatching from their eggs, young reptiles look exactly like their parents—but smaller. Many of them never see their parents. Most reptiles leave the eggs after laying them, so the babies must care for themselves.

Alligators and crocodiles carry their newly hatched young to the water, where the adults mostly live. They take care of their babies until they're able to live alone.

WORD WISE

EMBRYOS ARE UNBORN OR UNHATCHED LIVING THINGS IN THE PROCESS OF DEVELOPMENT.

Nesting

Birds lay their eggs in nests, which they make from objects such as grass, twigs, and mud. Their eggs have hard shells. Birds sit on the eggs to keep them warm while the embryos inside grow and get ready to hatch.

Some birds don't make nests. Emperor penguins live in Antarctica where there is nothing to make nests, so male penguins keep eggs warm by resting them on top of their feet.

A chick is often small, featherless, and helpless after hatching from an egg. Their parents keep them warm, bring them food, and protect them from other animals, such as eagles. Once the chicks grow feathers and grow larger and stronger, they are ready to leave the nest and fly away.

The common potoo lays one egg at a time on top of a broken branch. This way the bird can camouflage and hide the babies from possible predators.

compare and contrast

What are some similarities between the ways reptile and bird eggs are kept safe? What are the differences?

Some birds, such as songbirds, encourage their babies to leave the nest before they're ready in order to protect them from predators.

Live Births

Some animals are born the same way humans are. Mammals such as cats and apes develop inside the mother's body. By doing so, they can grow more fully before they are born. Fully developed babies are safer at birth than less-developed babies. For example, baby giraffes are ready to run just a few hours after being born—which would keep them safe if a predator was chasing them.

Many mammals, such as kittens, are born blind and deaf. Their eyes and ears open as they grow.

Orangutan mothers stay with their babies for six to seven years. Female orangutans are even known to "visit" their mothers until they reach the age of 15 or 16!

Mammal parents care for and protect their babies. A female mammal feeds her baby with milk from her body. This helps it to grow until it can feed itself. One or both parents protect the baby from danger. Oftentimes young mammals will stay with their parents until they're able to fend for, or take care of, themselves.

Consider This

Most mammals have fewer babies at a time than reptiles, but they care for them longer than reptiles. Why do you think they can do this?

Unique Mammals

Some mammals have unusual birth processes. Female kangaroos and other marsupials have short pregnancies of about six weeks. The embryo is born early and then continues to develop in a pouch on its mother's stomach. It feeds on milk, sleeps, and grows. A baby kangaroo might still hop back in its mother's pouch after leaving to keep warm and safe.

A joey is the name for a baby kangaroo.

A female duck-billed platypus lays eggs.

There are two unique mammals that lay eggs. Female spiny anteaters lay a single egg in a pouch. When the baby hatches, it feeds and grows to 500 times its original size. Then it leaves the pouch. A female duck-billed platypus lays an egg in a burrow, a kind of hole in the ground. The baby drinks its mother's milk after hatching.

Consider This

Why do scientists consider spiny anteaters and duck-billed platypuses to be mammals if they lay eggs? What other important features do they have?

Traveling Life

Certain living things travel as their life cycles progress. Salmon travel very far during their life cycle. Babies hatch from eggs in rivers and streams. Then they swim thousands of miles to the ocean. They grow and live in the ocean for up to seven years. When they're adults, they swim back to rivers and streams to mate and lay eggs.

A salmon dies after reproducing—thus completing its life cycle.

Sea turtles can travel more than 10,000 miles across the ocean to feed, mature, and lay eggs.

Some living things continue parts of their life cycle inside other creatures. Malaria **parasites** are so small we can't see them. When infected mosquitoes bite an animal to feed on its blood, malaria parasites swim from the mosquito's stomach into the victim's blood. Once in the bloodstream, parasites feed, grow, and reproduce inside of the animal that was bitten.

WORD WISE

PARASITES ARE LIVING THINGS THAT LIVE ON OR IN ANOTHER CREATURE AND BENEFIT FROM IT, WHILE OFTEN HARMING THE CREATURE ITSELF.

Final Stage

Death is the final stage of a living thing's life cycle. Some living things are born, grow, have young, and die rapidly. Some plants grow from seeds, grow flowers, and die in one season. A young mayfly hatches from an egg on the riverbed, living for up to two years underwater. It leaves the water as an adult. Some adults live for only 24 hours, but this is not always the case.

The leading cause of death among people in the world today is heart disease.

Many yareta plants are estimated to be over 3,000 years old.

Many animals live for a long time. Elephants can live for 70 years, and some humans live to be more than 100 years old. The yareta plant—found in the Atacama Desert in Chile—can live for centuries.

Consider This

Today, humans have a longer life expectancy than they did in the past. The global average life expectancy was 64 years old in 1990, and is 71 years old as of 2021. Why do you think humans are living longer now?

Unexpected Occurrences

Not every living thing can live a full life cycle—sometimes unexpected occurrences cause an early death. Some animals face danger from other animals. Lions hunt zebras, foxes eat rabbits, and bats eat flies. Plants die early in dry places where they can't get the water they need to make food. If a storm washes away a bird's nest, it can cause their early death.

Humans can also harm other living things. When people cut down trees to clear land for farms, animals lose their homes and food. When people kill mother elephants for their tusks, the baby elephants die. Other people help animals. They plant trees, try to stop hunting, or care for baby animals. It's important to help living things complete their life cycles!

Although they're both mammals, some foods that are common for humans to eat could kill their beloved pet dogs. Chocolate, onions, avocados, and grapes are each dangerous for a dog to eat.

compare and contrast

How are the dangers faced by animals similar to the dangers people face? How are they different?

Wildlife rescue groups wash and care for ducks that are affected by oil spills.

Glossary

alga A tiny organism that lives underwater and reproduces through photosynthesis.

camouflage Colors or shapes on animals that allow them to blend in with their surroundings.

develop The process of growing into something older or more mature.

environment All the physical surroundings on earth.

infect To spread an illness or disease to another living thing.

malaria A disease spread by mosquitoes.

mammal An animal that gives birth to live babies and feeds their young on milk from their body. Humans, dogs, and apes are examples of mammals.

marsupial A mammal that has a pouch on the mother's body in which their babies develop. Kangaroos are marsupials.

reproduce To create new individuals of the same kind.

unique Unlike others; out of the ordinary.

wetland Areas of land that hold a lot of water, such as swamps and marshes.

yolk Food found inside an egg. The yolk nourishes an embryo.

For More Information

Books

Gieseke, Tyler. *Plant and Animal Life Cycles*. Minneapolis, MN: DiscoverRoo, 2023.

Midthun, Joseph. *Animal Life Cycles*. Chicago, IL: World Book, 2022.

Murray, Lily. *How Old is a Whale? Animal Life Spans from the Mayfly to the Immortal Jellyfish*. Sommerville, MA: Big Picture Press, 2023.

Websites

National Geographic: How a Caterpillar Becomes a Butterfly: Metamorphosis, Explained
www.nationalgeographic.com/animals/article/science-of-metamorphosis-butterflies-caterpillars
Read more about a caterpillar's life from cocoon to butterfly.

National Geographic Kids: The Frog Life Cycle!
www.natgeokids.com/uk/discover/science/nature/frog-life-cycle/
Learn more about a frog's life cycle from tadpole to adult.

National Geographic Kids: The Life Cycle of Flowering Plants
www.natgeokids.com/uk/discover/science/nature/the-life-cycle-of-flowering-plants/
Learn more about pollination and seed dispersal.

Index

A

amphibian, 12, 13, 25

B

bird, 18, 19

C

camouflage, 19

D

death, 4, 26, 28, 29

E

egg, 10, 11, 13, 14, 15, 16, 17, 18, 19, 23, 25
embryo, 16, 17, 18, 22

F

fish, 14, 15, 24
flower, 6, 7, 8, 9, 26

G

gestation, 5

I

insect, 10, 11, 26

L

larva, 10
live birth, 20, 21

M

mammal, 20, 21, 22, 23, 27, 29
marsupial, 22
metamorphosis, 10, 11

N

nectar, 7
nest, 18, 19, 28
nymph, 11

P

parasite, 25
pollination, 6, 7
pupa, 10

R

reptile, 16, 17, 19

S

seed, 6, 8, 9, 26